Recurring Themes
In Education

P·C·P
Paul Chapman
Publishing Ltd

Paul Chapman Publishing Ltd
144 Liverpool Road
London
N1 1LA

British Library Cataloguing in Publication Data

Bruce, Tina
   Recurring Themes in Education
   I. Title
   370.1

ISBN 1-85396-264-3

Typeset by Dorwyn Ltd, Rowlands Castle, Hants
Printed and bound by The Baskerville Press, Salisbury, Wiltshire

A B C D E F G H   9 8 7 6 5

Contents

Acknowledgements

The earlier photographs are taken from the Early Childhood Collection
at the Froebel Institute College, Roehampton Institute, and Ibstock Place
School, the Froebel School. The photographs from the 1990s have been
taken by Margaret Sargent.

For the educators of tomorrow's children.

'. . . but if his philosophy is good and alive it will grow; and growing demands new, though always imperfect, forms for its expression.'

T.E. Campagnac (1934) The Permanent Value of Froebel's Teaching, *Child Life*, no. 162, p. 10.

The Historical Context

When Friedrich Froebel died in June 1852 at Marienthal, aged 70, the work to which he had devoted much of his life seemed to lie in ruins. A year before his death the 20 or so kindergartens which had been established throughout the German states had been proscribed by two decrees, a negative response by the authorities to the enlightened education that Froebel advocated which encouraged children to think for themselves, to question and to experiment, an education which put value on creativity and spontaneity and the development of the whole child. Faced with the upheaval of the 1848–9 revolution, the Prussian state reacted swiftly to suppress democratic movements and saw in Froebel's ideas the seeds of anarchy.

It had always been Froebel's wish to see his ideas extend beyond Germany and he both corresponded with like-minded acquaintances abroad and received visitors at his school at Keilhau and the kindergarten at Blankenburg, but he died too soon to witness the beneficial effects of this repression on the spread of his educational theories. The response of many liberal-minded Germans to the state's actions was to leave Germany for more tolerant countries and a number came to Britain from the late 1840s, bringing Froebel's ideas with them. Additionally, after Froebel's death, his second wife and former pupil, Luise Levin, and the Baroness von Marenholtz Bulow, who had been a proponent of Froebel's ideas since meeting him at Marienthal in 1849, both travelled extensively throughout Europe to promote the kindergarten philosophy.

The first kindergarten in England was opened in Hampstead in 1851 by Johannes and Berthe Ronge and moved to Tavistock Place in 1853. The couple came from Hamburg and had previously run a school and kindergarten there. Initially the kindergarten was for the children of German *émigrés* but as they became part of liberal middle-class society, so a demand arose for places for English children.

The first book published in England on kindergarten education, *A Practical Guide to the English Kindergarten*, was written by the Ronges in 1855 and followed a successful display of the Froebel Gifts and Occupations and associated lectures at the Society of Arts Educational Exhibition held in London in 1854. The examples of Froebel's Gifts and Occupations had been supplied by the Baroness von Marenholtz Bulow and for the duration of the exhibition the Tavistock Place kindergarten was open to the public.

During the following 20 years the kindergarten movement slowly gained ground, attracting the approval of such figures as Charles Dickens, who was a frequent visitor at the Tavistock Place kindergarten, Mrs Gaskell, Charles Keen and Rowland Hill. Favourable comments on kindergarten education began to appear in the reports of the inspectors appointed by the government to visit infant and elementary schools in receipt of state funding. The Rev. Muirhead Mitchell, HMI for church schools in the eastern counties, went so far as to advise teachers to contact the Ronges to obtain the Gifts and Occupations.

The kind of education provided in state schools was slowly becoming recognised as inappropriate for the very young compared to the activities offered in the private kindergartens. Infant schools frequently had anything from 50 to 100 children imprisoned in rows of seats rising in tiers from the central desk of the master or mistress. This gallery form of classroom organisation necessarily prohibited individual work and was only suitable for whole-class teaching, usually by rote.

One reason for the slow development of the kindergarten movement was the decision of some of the German *émigrés* to return home once the restraints on democratic activity were relaxed in the early 1860s. Johannes and Berthe Ronge were one such couple, although Johannes had applied for, and was granted, a certificate of naturalisation, on the basis of his intention to carry on his educational work in England. However, a sufficient number remained behind to work with the growing band of English adherents to ensure gradual growth and contact was maintained with the international network which had come into being.

The danger was that with very few English language texts on kindergarten practice, and no translations of Froebel's own writings, his ideas would become misunderstood and open to misrepresentation. Kindergartens could be opened by anyone with only the most vague idea of Froebel's philosophy and bad practice could result in the movement falling into disrepute. What was needed was an organisation devoted to the propagation of Froebel's ideas and, eventually, in 1874, this came about with the formation of the Froebel Society.

The lack of suitably trained teachers for her new kindergarten in London led Miss Beata Doreck, who had lived in London since her arrival from Württemberg in 1857, to propose to like-minded acquaintances the creation of a Kindergarten Association. The first meeting was held at her home in Kensington Gardens in November 1874 and was attended by 18 people, including visiting German Froebelians Madame Althaus and Fraulein Roth, Madame Emilie Michaelis, who had recently arrived to take up residence in London, and Fraulein Eleonore Heerwart. Fraulein Heerwart had worked in kindergartens in Manchester, Belfast and Dublin and was visiting London prior to returning to Germany. The developments taking place encouraged her to remain in England and she accepted a post as Principal of the Kindergarten Training Department at Stockwell College, established by the British and Foreign School Society, in September 1874.

It is in the Minute Books of the Froebel Society that we can trace the development of policy and these date from that first preliminary meeting held on 4 November 1874. The decision to call the new organisation the Kindergarten Association drew criticism from Froebelians in Manchester where the movement had already established strong roots. In 1873 the Manchester Kindergarten Association had been formed and it was felt that a new London-based society with a similar name would lead to confusion. At a meeting held in London in February 1875 a large majority voted in favour of the The Froebel Society for the Promotion of the Kindergarten System.

Discussion at this meeting also centred on the questions of publicity and the availability of texts on Froebel and kindergarten education. It was resolved to ask the editor of the Women's Education Union Journal to publish reports of the society meetings and at the following meeting in March 1875 it was recorded that this journal was prepared not only to print monthly reports but also to include a list of kindergarten books prepared by the society.

Another aspect of the work of the society was the need to provide an approved scheme of training for kindergarten teachers, as a variety of courses existed both in training colleges and in private establishments. As early as October 1875 an examinations committee was formed to draw up a syllabus for a Froebel Society Certificate. This particular work of promoting a unified system for examination and a joint certificate was taken over by the Joint Examination Board, representing the Froebel Society, the Manchester Kindergarten Association and, later, the Bedford Kindergarten Association. The National Froebel Union came into being in 1887 and took over the role of administering examinations in 1888. The Froebel movement in England now had two distinct branches, with the Froebel Society retaining responsibility for the propaganda activities – establishing training courses including lecture courses and evening classes at all levels, holding summer schools, promoting publication of books, articles and pamphlets and liaising with other educational organisations and with the Board of Education.

The society recognised the central importance of providing English-language commentaries on kindergarten education, either written by English practitioners or translated from German texts, and members of the committee of the Froebel Society were active in both fields. Emily Shirreff, the society's President from 1875 to 1897, published *The Kindergarten at Home: A Practical Handbook for Mothers*, in 1882, as well as a biographical sketch of Froebel's life and an exposition of the principles of Froebelian education. Mary Gurney produced an abridged translation of August Koehler's *Praxis de Kindergartens*, with the approval of the author, and this was published in two parts under the title *Kindergarten Practice*, (2nd edn, 1877). One of the founder members of the society, Emilie Michaelis, who was later to be the first Principal of the Froebel Educational Institute, and H. Keatley Moore, the society's Treasurer for many years, edited Froebel's letters. These were published as *Froebel's Letters on the Kindergarten* in 1891 and followed their earlier translation of Froebel's *Autobiography* in 1886.

The publication of pamphlets and lectures was a convenient way of publicising Froebel's ideas in a succinct form. In the nineteenth century these tended to be on general principles of kindergarten practice, for example Emily Shirreff's *The Kindergarten in Relation to Schools* and E.A. Manning's *Froebel and*

Infant Training (1884). In this century they have been more concerned with specific aspects of the curriculum, such as Margaret Hutchinson's *Practical Nature Study in Town Schools*, which explores ways in which a key Froebelian subject can be adapted to a different environment, and *Mathematics in the Primary School* by Margaret Ironside and Sheila Roberts.

Another way of promoting knowledge of Froebelian ideas was through the publication of a journal and the society made its first venture in this area in January 1883 with *The Journal of the Froebel Society*. This was intended to be a 'small monthly issue, which will give a slight but regular report of what is doing to keep before those who are not students the leading principles of the admirable system we have bound ourselves together to unfold and promote'. This attempt to publish a journal ended 13 issues later in January 1884 but, for the period of its duration, it provided subscribers with articles, book reviews, notice of lectures and a forum for correspondence. As with so many of the society's activities, it was financial pressure which brought the venture to an end.

The society next pursued the idea of a journal in December 1890 when the council resolved to use *Child Life*, which was to be launched in January 1891 by George Philip & Son, as 'the medium of communication among the subscribers of the Froebel Society'. From its inception it carried reports of the society's meetings, details of lecture series, notification of examination arrangements and general news about the progress of the kindergarten movement. This journal was discontinued in 1892 but the title was taken over, with the permission of the publisher, by the Michaelis Guild, the alumni organisation for past students of the Froebel Educational Institute, for the magazine published in 1897. In the meantime the Froebel Society had used *Hand and Eye* as a medium for communication among its members. To add to the confusion the Froebel Society decided to make another attempt at publishing its own journal in 1899 and adopted the title *Child Life*. The first edition of this journal, which continued under this name until 1939, was published in January 1899.

The need to promote Froebelian ideas beyond the kindergarten stage had long been recognised by the society. Froebel's philosophy did not extend solely to the very young but envisaged an ideal education as one which continued throughout life. This resulted in a change of title for the society in 1917 to the Froebel Society and Junior Schools Association.

The next major change in the society came in 1938 when the two branches of the Froebel movement decided to combine, after years of separate and not always harmonious existence. The amalgamation of the Froebel Society and the National Froebel Union into the National Froebel Foundation (NFF) took place after some years of discussion and negotiation, and the first meeting of the combined body was held in November 1938. This reunification enabled the Froebel movement to continue its work on a united front in response to the realities of twentieth-century educational policy and in the face of continuing financial constraints. The new organisation took the opportunity to rename its journal, and the title *Child Life* finally disappeared and was replaced by the *National Froebel Foundation Bulletin* from January 1940. However, as time went on, the NFF found it increasingly difficult to maintain a steady flow of articles for the bimonthly bulletin and, finally, in March 1965, the *Froebel Journal* was launched in its place as a termly publication. The demise of the *Froebel Journal* in autumn 1974 came just over a year before the final meeting of the NFF governors in November 1975. However the NFF is still in existence, presided over by a board of trustees which actively promotes Froebel's philosophy by sponsoring appropriate research and publications, particularly in the field of early childhood education.

In *Recurring Themes in Education*, the articles discussed have been taken from the journals and pamphlets published by the National Froebel Society/ NFF between 1899 and 1974. The original sources are held in the NFF archive housed at Templeton, headquarters of the Incorporated Froebel Educational Institute, and in the Early Childhood Collection at Froebel Institute College, now a constituent college of the Roehampton Institute, both in London. The NFF archives and the Early Childhood Collection are open to *bona fide* researchers and inquiries should be made to the archivist.

The way this book came to be written is described in more detail in the section 'About this book', which follows.

About this Book

This book was written at the suggestion of the National Froebel Foundation. Any interpretations are those of the authors, and not necessarily those of the trustees. The aim was to make a book providing a modern perspective to Froebelian philosophy using his writings and extracts of archive material which would be of relevance to educators working in the last decade of the century. The authors set to work, with the aim of opening up the archive material in ways which will hold meaning for educators of today.

This book is an attempt to continue the dialogue and, it is hoped, to raise future research questions which, if funding permits, might be acted upon. Most important for the authors of this book is the attempt to work with children in the light of new knowledge, and constantly and regularly to juxtapose traditional Frobelian ideals against this. This book aims to lead educators onwards and into the next century. Vision is an important part of being an educator, but it must always be grounded in real situations. Educators in general, but Froebelians in particular, will need to do some deep studying and learning in order to develop effective practical strategies if they are to be useful to children, their families and their educators in the future.

Much of the material in the archives should be allowed to gather dust. However there are, among the multitude of articles, some, which if known about, would be of interest and use to the modern educator. The most striking feature is the way that each generation of educators seems to deal with issues which emerge again and again. This is important for a number of reasons. History can, if we use it as a resource, help us to find ways forward in educational thinking and practice. We can avoid working through the reinvention of the wheel with each new generation of educators. By knowing that educators before us have encountered the same difficulties, we will not feel so burdened or isolated. By knowing where we are coming from we can contextualise our work, so that it is well grounded in a consistent philosophical approach supported by current theory and research evidence. This empowers the educator to move forward with a sense of direction.

In Britain, the impact of Froebel's philosophy on primary education has been enormous. During the last two decades this influence has not taken such a high profile. However it is still evident in government documents (such as DES, 1990, and the *Start Right* Report (Ball, 1994) funded by the RSA).

This book will help readers to see that there are central issues which need to be tackled again and again, and about which educators need to be clear. When there is conceptual confusion about these fundamental concerns, important ground is lost in educating young children in ways which demonstrate quality. The book is not concerned with returning to a past golden era when Froebelian philosophy flourished. It is about teasing out central educational issues, which each generation of educators needs to address as they inevitably recur. It is about finding quality ways forward in relation to these, which honour the past without being straitjacketed by it.

The archive material is used to identify and reflect on the recurring themes. There is analysis and commentary linking these with the way the same recurring themes impinge nowadays. This means that there will be parallels between past and present throughout the book, but also emphasis on the need for educators to keep rethinking fundamental issues according to the era in which they are functioning. Thus quality in primary education can be both protected and developed without erosion, loss or ossification.

It is only natural for educators of each generation to seek out and enjoy the company of those colleagues with whom they agree on matters of education. They will inevitably want to talk with those who hold dear the same philosophical framework as they do. This allows a feeling of security and well-being. It reaffirms the work being practised with children and their families. As educators do this they are in fact taking an opportunity to find words through which to communicate, share, clarify, find evidence for and rehearse the arguments for their deeply held educational beliefs. It also empowers them to face those with whom they disagree.

While it is usual to home in on like-minded educators among contemporaries, it is not so usual to use archive material as a mechanism for meeting the minds, thoughts and reflections of colleagues from earlier times. Colleagues from the past will, of course, word things differently, but it is the basic sharing of ideas and educational approach across time which is the fascination of the authors of this book.

Presumably all those who were invited to contribute to *Child Life*, the *National Froebel Foundation Bulletin* and the *Froebel Journal* were asked to do so because they were seen as having an approach which was basically in tune with Froebelian values. It is interesting to let our modern-day thoughts on education interact with those of our predecessors. They can help us to sharpen our thinking, and so move forward to a better educational future. We are likely to find that the old cliché is true. There are no new ideas in education. We can worry in case we inevitably go round and round in circles, stuck for ever in a groove. Perhaps this is a serious defect in the human mind: the limits of the individual are set by the limits of the species. However, human minds are probably more flexible than they are sometimes encouraged to be. When challenged to do so, human thinking can move forwards in leaps and bounds. After all, the human brain is not functioning in isolation from the environment in which it operates. The environment is made up of people, time, space and physical materials, all of which have a huge impact on the human brain in all its aspects. This means that humans are capable of making changes and adjustments as situations demand. For nothing stays exactly as it has been. Both humans and their circumstances inevitably keep changing.

Any recurring theme meets a different environment and context each time it recurs. It can never be exactly the same twice. Those who deny, ignore, dismiss or even ridicule the importance of looking back in order to look forward are iconoclastic revolutionaries. They bulldoze and destroy, with frightening speed, what has gone before. They purport to do this in the name of progress. Others, like the authors of this book, will prefer a different course. They will hoard and keep old ideas, many of which will quite rightly never see the light of day again. But some ideas, themes and issues will be used again. Those that do will be the recurring themes which cannot help but surface at regular intervals.

Keeping a steady course is very different from revolution, which means constantly reinventing the wheel and using up massive amounts of human energy in doing so. By juxtaposing current ideas, theory and research with a time-honoured recurrent theme, it is possible to see where and in what ways it remains useful and where recent thinking has modified or extended what it can offer in terms of helping educators to work optimally with children and families. Taking account of the past and using it means continuity with progression, rather than revolution and stop-start ways of working with different factions rising and falling.

Throughout history there has been the problem of paradigm shift. Educators fall in love with the research and theories they have most used to guide their practice. As soon as educators look at recurring themes, they have a good mechanism to help them adopt new research and theory, while keeping continuity through the unchanging nature of the scheme. It also saves them from the disillusion of finding a theory they are using is wrong or outmoded. Some dismiss theory at this point: 'Everything I learnt at college has since been proved wrong. So why bother with theory?' It would be more constructive to say, the theory through which we examine a certain theme is found wanting. Any theory is the product of the human imagination, and will therefore not last forever. How did colleagues from the past tackle this one? Is there anything here for us?

The remarkable thing is that there always seems to be something in it for us now. It is not a case of going back. It is a case of taking what is still useful forward.

The Structure of the Book

Each chapter in this book has a similar format:

- It begins with a quotation from Froebel's thinking in W.N. Hailmann's (1887) translation from the original German of *The Education of Man*, which introduces one of six recurring themes in education.
- It is followed by an introduction to the selected articles in the Early Childhood Collection at the Froebel Institute College, and the NFF archive at Templeton. Articles have been chosen because of their relationship with the theme focused upon in a particular chapter.
- Then follows the article itself, sometimes edited and sometimes in full.
- The chapter is completed by a commentary on the recurring theme in education, using the archive article and referring to wider forward-looking sources.

The six themes chosen are:

1. Are children fundamentally good?
2. What is the process of development?
3. How can development be best augmented?
4. What activates development and turns it into learning?
5. How supportive is the structure of education for the child's development and learning?
6. What gives a teacher inspiration?

THEME 1:

Are Children Fundamentally Good?

The only infallible remedy for counteracting any shortcomings and even wickedness is to find the originally good sources, the originally good side of the human being that has been repressed, disturbed or misled into the shortcoming, and then to foster, build up and properly guide this good side. Thus the shortcoming will at last disappear, although it may involve a hard struggle against habit, but not against original depravity in man.

(Froebel, 1887, pp. 121–2)

INTRODUCTION

It is sometimes said that recurring themes in education come round every 30 years or so, and that seeing a theme re-emerge for the second time is a sign of advancing age for an educator. Hence the weary cry, 'but we've been here before!' The point about a recurring theme in education is that the basic issues surrounding it remain and crop up time and again. Different people, at different points in history, in different places, will, as night follows day, address a question like the first recurring theme in this book. Are children fundamentally good or bad? It is an inevitable part of life's experience to consider a question such as this, either directly or, more usually, implicitly. The decisions conscious or subconscious that are made in answer to this question will have a huge impact on the way adults work with children. It is preferable if recurring themes can be raised to a conscious level so that they can receive the detailed scrutiny they both deserve and need.

Badley, in relation to this theme, emphasises goodness rather than badness. His focus is on self-development and self-expression, and the way these develop to embrace a sense of others, and of community. He assumes that children are naturally inclined towards goodness, so much so that he sees self-development and self-expression as leading towards this.

Badley has raised an old chestnut in his article. He aligns himself with the Froebelian quotation at the beginning of the chapter. Down the years from Froebel's time in the nineteenth century to the turn of the century when Froebelians and Montessorians fought fierce battles in the UK, to the build up

1

to the Second World War, when Badley worked, and to the late 1980s when the National Curriculum was introduced by law, the question of how good or bad children are has been an issue for educators. The Froebelians and Montessorians might have had areas of strong disagreement, but not in this matter. As far as they are concerned, children are born with a tendency to goodness, which needs to be encouraged and nurtured. The National Curriculum, introduced into Scotland, England, Wales and N. Ireland in different forms from 1989, itself is neutral in this area, but the notion of inspection and testing of children to enforce them (and their teachers) not to slack (because of a tendency to badness?) is anything but neutral. It has led to fierce debate among educators, school governors, politicians and parents.

Badley's article is useful because four areas emerge from it. These facilitate reflection on the important issue of whether or not children are fundamentally good or bad:

1. The first area Badley's article raises is the question: 'What is meant by being good or being bad?'
2. The second area in relation to the question of whether or not children are fundamentally good or bad is about the need, or not, to place limits on what children do regardless of whether or not they are inclined to be good or bad.
3. The third area relevant to thoughts around goodness or badness is whether adults need to mould bad children into good shape, or whether good citizens are produced by the cultivation of what is seen by proponents of this approach as a natural inclination to grow into good people. The gardening imagery of the second approach is significant. The way, the process, by which children are encouraged in their goodness is all important. Moulding smacks of habit formation and passivity on the part of the learner, in order to have the desired result or product. Cultivation, by contrast, suggests not so much a product but more a process with active adults and active children learning autonomously.
4. The fourth area suggests not only the need to establish whether or not children are basically one or the other but also to consider whether that decision should be the prerogative of parents, religious organisations, of educators in the schools, or of central government.

There has been a battle for the hearts, minds and souls of children throughout the centuries and particularly since the inception of state education in the UK in the 1870s. These were issues in Froebel's day, issues in 1938 and remain issues for today.

FREEDOM IN EDUCATION Badley, J.H. (1938) Freedom in
èducation – IV: The purpose of freedom and ways of achieving it.
Child Life, Vol. IV, no. 1, pp. 2–5. (J.H. Badley was the Headmaster of
Bedales School.)

To some in the first flush of freedom, education may appear to be a process of liberation from restraints and complexes, giving freedom for unhindered growth. To be rid of harmful or unnecessary restrictions is so far good, but if freedom is to have its full value it must be something more as well. The purpose of discipline, as has been said, is to establish limits within which we can be free – to provide that 'enclosed space' without which freedom can so easily become dangerous licence. But the enclosed space is only a mockery if it is left empty or only to be used as a drill ground.

To give freedom, it must resemble not a barrack yard but a garden, full of things that arouse wonder and love, and that afford delightful possibilities of discovery and creative occupation. It is this provision of opportunity that is the positive aspect of freedom, the importance of which is apt to be overlooked. Little is gained by the absence of repressions if the only result is an untenanted void.

The parable of the 'house swept and garnished' is a piece of true psychology. It is possible to drive out the one devil of repression, only to make room for seven others of aimlessness and self-will, and the last state of the child brought up in completer absence of restrictions may be worse than the first.

We have, in short, to learn to think not so much of what there is freedom from as of what there is freedom for, and to realise that if the freedom that is given by release from harmful and irksome restrictions is important, still more important is the 'freedom for' that is given by opportunity.

Freedom of opportunity

There could scarcely be a better example of this than a good Nursery School, where the children are human beings in their own right and are treated as such. There they enjoy a greater fullness of life, with lots of interest and beauty in their surroundings, a world of friendly companionship with plenty to do – activities that, however irksome they might be if the children had the feeling that they were being made to do them, become pleasant when they find that they are doing them of their own accord and in company with others who are also enjoying them. This is the real sense of freedom.

An abundance of mental and spiritual nourishment is given which is not only satisfying but appetising, given in a way and at a time that make it attractive, so that the children have the feeling in all that they do, not of acting under compulsion, but because they like it.

It is because of careful organisation and loving guidance that in such a school so large an amount of freedom is possible. And this is the teacher's main function – to provide abundant material of all kinds that will arouse and satisfy the desire for activity, within a general framework of organisation and discipline that is necessary if there is to be the fullest freedom. It is not our function as educators to try and mould children to a pattern. We are there to provide the garden within which they can grow most freely and most naturally to be themselves, and to be their best selves.

Variety of interest

Freedom in school, then, means abundant opportunity. In this connection it is important to give a good proportion of the school day to the arts and craft work. All children need experience of this kind for the full development of all sides of their nature, and there are many who find the possibility of development through these interests and through activities of this kind rather than in any of the more abstract studies. Every encouragement should be given to the child's creative instinct, to his desire to do something for himself. Moreover, he should have the opportunity of making things that have an intelligible meaning, and a use and beauty for him at the time, and not in preparation for a future that he cannot yet realise. That is why all school work at first, and much throughout, should be the actual taking part in arts and crafts; stories that kindle the imagination; play that represents earlier phases of human life or foreshadows later; projects that can take practical shape; and any way of dramatising knowledge that makes of it a real actual experience.

The use of tools

The thing that most of all, with the exception of connected speech, has marked man off from the other animals, and enabled him to rise so far above them is his use of tools. Speech and the use of tools have been the chief means of education of mankind, and must always be so. If we keep this in mind, we shall not be likely to underrate the training value to be found in handling tools. Even young children can become surprisingly skilful in this direction, and can make things from which they get intense pleasure and a training of the utmost value.

When reading and writing are approached as giving tools of another kind, and books are regarded as store rooms of material out of which, by the use of the new tools, all manner of things of use and beauty can be got, there is here a vast extension of mastery, creativity and delight. Every such extension of opportunity makes those to whom it comes more free. It brings a means of escape from limitations of ignorance and powerlessness, and opens up another pathway into a world of delight, where, as the learner advances, there is continually more to do and more to want to do.

The question of choice

If we want to give the fullest opportunity, and to have it used to the full, we shall be careful to see that the training on which we insist is not all routine, or all activity in which there is no choice. This does not mean that children are to be allowed to choose whether they will come to lessons or not. They cannot be allowed to choose whether they will learn any given subject – say arithmetic – or not. They have not yet enough experience, either of their requirements of life or of their own capacities to make such a choice at this stage, though later on it will be possible and necessary for them to decide whether they will take mathematics, say, as a special line of study.

There is a certain groundwork both of skill and knowledge that is essential for any civilised life, and this should gradually become a part of their experience, first in play, and then through practical problems of all kinds, so naturally that the question of choice does not arise in connection with this or that subject of study, but only now and then in regard to the way of dealing with it.

Individual needs

A strong advocate of freedom in education, Bertrand Russell, has urged that children ought not to be made to come to classes that do not interest them, on the grounds that if teachers found their classes dwindling, they might then amend their teaching methods. Though the falling off of numbers might act as a good interest-meter, it might not improbably lead at times to the substitution of amusement for sound teaching. So far as the child is concerned however, it supposes that he has an accurate knowledge of his own needs, and a soundness of judgement that he does not always possess.

At the same time full allowance should be made for individual differences, especially in the range of interests included in the school course, and in the encouragement of hobbies. The school curriculum might be compared to a pyramid, with a wide base, so that every child may have full opportunity to try out his powers and discover what he can do best, and what he most enjoys doing. Thus we begin to see what he is best fitted for.

The range of work would then gradually narrow down for each individual, as his natural bent and the requirements of his career might determine. Education should never be allowed to be too vocational in character.

Training which has in view from the first a particular kind of adult occupation may produce a high degree of efficiency, but it will be efficiency within a narrow range, to the loss of potentialities that might have found their satisfaction in activities of greater value both to the individual and the community.

Ample opportunity should be given also for recreational activities and the pursuit of hobbies of every kind, where again a wide field of choice should be given.

The emotional life

Freedom must also be sought in the emotional life, and opportunity given for expression of the affections. School life is too apt to be one long repression of natural feeling, which is either permanently dulled and stunted by lack of nourishment and exercise, or else driven inward to form an unsatisfied complex, or forced to find expression in some unwholesome form. The cultivation of beauty, and the care of beautiful things in the surroundings of the children have an important influence in this respect. An atmosphere of friendliness, and opportunity for affectionate comradeship are essential.

One of the advantages of a co-educational school is that boys and girls grow up together, on terms of complete equality. In their daily intercourse in their work and play, in their interests and amusements, their emotional development finds the food and exercise it needs, and is more natural than if it is starved or forced into some unwholesome channel.

To this feeling of freedom in comradeship, and comradeship in freedom, any sort of co-operative effort can contribute. Stage plays, orchestral and choral music, societies of the pursuit of some common interest, and all forms of common service to the community – all these activities which lie outside the 'usual school subjects' are no less valuable, and no less essential a part of education, as helping to provide that wealth of opportunity which is the positive aspect of freedom.

Freedom and government

With regard to the question of government, if the fullest freedom of the individual is the purpose we have in mind, then the ideal theory of government is that held by the anarchists. To these all government is bad, because it cannot fail in some particulars, and in some cases, to be oppressive and to arouse resentment, and so the less of it the better. Such a theory is indeed ideal, since it presupposes a state of things such as has never yet existed, but it is not, while human nature remains imperfect, a practicable ideal in any normal community, whether this be a state or a school. It is, however, an ideal well worth keeping in mind as one towards which to work.

Perhaps the nearest approach to the anarchist's ideal is to be seen in a good nursery school, where there is very little of the machinery of government visible. Where everything is planned and carried through for the good of the children, government is a benevolent despotism, so benevolent that it is not felt. Such a form of government, however, which is appropriate in the earliest stages of education, is not ideal in the later stages. It produces a willing compliance, without the sense of compulsion or restriction, and establishes good habits. These are good as far as they go. But to those who regard freedom of development as worth far more than obedience, however willing, or habit however good, this is, except as a stage of growth, a false idea of government.

Full opportunity for growth, and the best possible conditions for promoting it must be provided, but growth itself can come only from within the children themselves. It is just here that both kinds of despotism, that of authority and that of benevolence are apt to fail, because they fall short of the main purpose of education, which is the encouragement of self-development by means of self-activity.

With every advance of age, and with the development of a more critical judgement, the question of government will become more insistent. The time will inevitably come when the need of rules and their efficacy will be questioned. How is this questioning to be met? The answer has always been by discipline, and this answer, I believe, is right.

As long as there are in the community those who have not yet attained to full development, we cannot do without discipline. It is essential to have some form of government, and to have those whose duty is to see that order is kept and justice done. The mistake lies in forgetting that these are not ends in themselves, but only means to an end, and in failing to use them as such. If the end they are to serve is the fullest possible development of the individual with a growing apprehension of the values of mind and spirit and a growing power of self-direction in accordance with these values, it is plain that such can be achieved only if there is a continuous development from external authority through various degrees of self-government towards an ideal in which government ceases to be necessary. Spontaneity of impulse together with self-control, rather than a habit of mechanical obedience, are the outcome and criterion of a true education.

Self-government

It is impossible to pass from the stage of benevolent despotism to a system of complete self-government at a bound. What matters is that there should be a growth from habit to conscious choice, and that whatever choice is possible should be real, carrying responsibility for its results, for freedom always involves responsibility. That is why it is right to ask children, when they make their own rules, also to help to see that they are carried out. Without wise guidance any experiment of the kind may easily result in mere disorder, and may only serve to bring the whole principle of self-government into discredit, but because in the wrong hands it does not work, this does not prove that no kind of self-government is to be attempted.

By self-government in the school, therefore, I do not mean either on the one side an entire absence of rules and a state of *laissez-faire,* which leaves much to chance, and allows experience to be bought at the cost of harm to oneself and others, nor yet, on the other side, any system of government on the military pattern, in which some of the rank and file are invested with authority as non-commissioned officers. What I would have is a continually increasing amount of self-government that takes two forms: the one, acceptance of responsibility of some kind, no matter how small at first, and enlarging with growth in age and powers, looked upon as service undertaken for the welfare of the whole community in helping to carry out the common purpose of the school; and the other, a growing understanding of its aims and needs through the give-and-take of discussion, and a growing share in the making and administration of its rules, so that what in the early stages begins as habits may develop into voluntary acceptance and conscious purpose.

That, I hold, is one of the main things education has to do, whether we regard it as concerned with the full development of the individual during the actual years of growth, or as preparation for meeting the demands, and utilising the opportunities that adult life will bring.

The choice today

This brings us back to the choice that faces us today, between the claims of the authoritarian state to shape our lives and our thoughts to its service, and some form of political and social life in which freedom of thought and action is possible, and in which we can take part, not as cogs in a machine, but as human beings possessed of freewill. Which is it to be? Those who believe in force, as the source of authority and the ultimate appeal think that the question can be settled by bombs and machine guns.

In a way it can. Force can crush and kill and produce obedience and an outward show of order, but the one thing that force cannot do is to make life. And it is with life and growth that we as educators are concerned, not merely with obedience and order. It is we who are responsible for the choice, for the question will be settled ultimately, not on the battlefield but in the school.

The choice is being made all the time, not only by what we teach and how we teach it, but by the habits we establish, the motives to which we appeal, the ideals we uphold, and most of all by the subconscious ideals and motives – those complex wholes of thought and feeling – which are the outcome of experience that has been lived.

In the formation of these ideals, our own belief in the value of authority and freedom, and our understanding of their use, will be a factor, perhaps the most powerful factor of all.

The greatest of these is –

I have been insisting mainly on the need of freedom for self-development and self-expression. That is a fundamental urge of life. But there is also another urge, of which love in all its forms is a manifestation. This is no less fundamental, and leads further still. Both of these are urges to freedom. Both seek to escape the limits and letting the self grow greater, the other by breaking through them and merging the self in communion with other selves and with the whole of which we are a part. The one is a freedom that makes for power, but this is only a poor and partial freedom if it does not lead on to the fuller freedom which is found in unselfish love.

COMMENTARY

What it means to be good or bad

Being good or bad has nothing to do with belief in a god or gods. It is not linked with organised religion of any kind. However, those steeped in religious beliefs, and perhaps also belonging to an organised religion, will often argue that it is helpful to have a clearly set-out code of conduct so that inner held values are acted upon in everyday life. Within the Christian religion, it is perhaps Quakers who take this to the furthest, believing that the way people live their lives closely reflects their inner values. Sir Michael Rutter (1983) is helpful here in teasing out how this impacts on Froebel's central attitudes, values and philosophy. For Rutter there is a very thin line between some Quakers and agnostics. The difference is the leap of faith to belief in God as opposed to belief in goodness.

Froebel, born in the eighteenth century, was a man of his time, and Christian religious ideas were part of his thinking and experience of life. He was steeped in Christianity, although his love of nature and work as a forester affected him in a way which is at times almost pantheistic. The interesting thing for us in the twentieth century is that, like Rutter, Froebel believed the most important thing is the way in which we live as a reflection of our inner beliefs. A god or gods may or may not be the inspiration behind this. To Froebel, God was an important force in his belief that children are fundamentally good.

It is through the goodness of God that children are born naturally inclined to be good. They come to know about God, and they come to know about goodness in a fuller sense. Life requires that we make decisions, which are often in reality moral judgements (Brearley, 1969 p. 139). Sometimes actions are not in tune with moral decisions. However, people often and regularly do put the common good before the selfish one. A good person lives by principles, such as justice, integrity or respect for persons, in ways which go beyond personal gain. When the crunch comes, for most people it is easier to put others known and loved before self than it is to put first others who are neither known nor loved. Going without a new, much-needed coat is easier for a mother if it means new shoes for her own children, but not so easy if it means food for a starving child in another part of the world.

Goodness is to do with respect for others. However, it also includes respect for self. Badley touches on this: 'I have been insisting on the need for freedom of self-development and self-expression.' He also places great emphasis on 'the fuller freedom which is found in unselfish love'. Badley has caught the essence of goodness as perceived by Froebel in the quotation at the beginning of the chapter. Goodness has a fundamental urge to escape the limitations of self. 'By enlarging these limits and letting the self grow greater, and the other by breaking through them and merging the self in communion with other selves and with the whole of which we are a part.'

In other words, goodness and badness are about the relationship with oneself, and also of self and society. This is further explored in *Theme 6* which looks at Froebel's concept of the principle of unity. In Badley's view, young children do not have enough experience of what life requires of them, or of what they can manage in order to be given complete freedom of choice. However he does say 'school is too apt to be one long repression of natural feeling'. It is important to look at this remark through the distinction Alan Blyth (1988, p. 20) draws between two kinds of informal education. The first type stresses interpersonal equality and freedom of thought and expression in the way espoused by Badley and Froebel before him. The second type of informal education, which is closely linked with social and political ideas of the left, is a stark contrast. It aims to develop a collectivist culture in which to enable a socialist society.

Proponents of the right, in Blyth's view rarely distinguish between these two kinds of informal education. This is demonstrated in the slogan:

> The progressives have had their say,
> The progressives have had their way,
> The progressives have had their day.

This emphasises the second type of informal education, not the first, which Badley and other Froebelians as well as Montessorians and Steinerians espouse (Bruce, 1987 p. 32). Typically, the two are fused in this comment.

The repression to which Badley refers is a criticism of authoritarian limits being placed on children. However, while he may not favour military-style discipline, he is very clear that 'there is little gained by the absence of repression if the only result is an untenanted space'. For Froebel and Badley, freedom does not mean no limits or boundaries being placed on children. Neither support the view that children should do as they please, for that leads to untenanted space, in which children are likely to feel insecure, and to flounder. Children need opportunities to be free without the 'dangerous licence' of no limits. He believes schools can make a valuable contribution in this. Freedom to learn does not mean in his terms 'an untenanted void'.

Some aspects of learning require the help of those who are already competent and understanding of them. Some things need to be actively taught, or children will not be able to learn them. Here Badley is anticipating Bruner's thinking in the 1960s, that adults are the scaffolding that links the child with knowledge and understanding. Bruner (1977, p. xiv) suggests that human children have particularly long childhoods compared with other mammals, precisely because there is so much they need to learn and be taught in order to fully function as adults.

Without realising it, for the work had not then been translated into English, Badley is also linking with Vygotsky. Vygotsky wrote in the 1930s of a zone of potential development. In his view the adult, or older more experienced and competent peer, helps the younger child to function in advance of actual development. For example, by reading Rosemary Sutcliff's *Roman Trilogy* to a 7-year-old, a story too difficult for the child to read alone, it can be both enjoyed and appreciated. Later, at 14 years of age, the adolescent can enjoy reading this independently.

Just as children need teachers who are trained to help them learn, so they need to attend lessons. According to Badley, there cannot be an option here. Learning is not a matter of going to lessons for the sake of being amused. All learning has an element of struggle in it. Children need skilled help in learning to struggle with things difficult, as they learn to use tools of all kinds (Bruce, 1991, p. 84).

The arts, crafts, reading, writing, beautiful surroundings, a friendly atmosphere, feeling part of a community, trying to do things for oneself and creating things, all contribute. Within these basic experiences, all of which children need, adults can offer options and the encouragement of self-chosen hobbies.

Badley makes it clear that he believes self-respect to be important. His basic curriculum approach demonstrates the symbiotic relationship among self, community and society at large.

He adds play to the curriculum for the youngest children. Looking at his reasons for doing so, it becomes clear how far research and theory have moved forward since 1938. At that time, Freudian theory was the main influence, whereas in the 1990s a wider range of theoretical influence has had an impact on the justification of including play in the early childhood curriculum.

Moulding children into goodness, or cultivating the goodness that is already in them

Whatever education systems as a whole emphasise, there will always be those who keep a steady course. Many educators, but Froebelians in particular, in each generation have always stressed the inherent goodness in children, and are likely to continue to do so whether or not the climate favours this approach. In a few decades' time it will be interesting to see if the late 1980s and 1990s are regarded as periods when the education system as a whole accented the positive or the negative attributes of children as learners.

Those who are inclined to see children as good in essence have a tendency, metaphorically speaking, to place them in gardens, and to cultivate, weed and encourage healthy growth from unfolding bud to flower. In contrast, those who believe children are naturally inclined to be bad want to place them in settings which will firmly (gently, it is hoped) mould them into shape, the shape that adults require. Throughout the history of British education, people have argued with equal passion the strength of taking up one or the other of these approaches. This recurring theme runs very deep indeed. Because it touches on aspects of a person's philosophy of life, it is not surprising that it arouses passionate feelings about what is the best way to work with a child, and who should make the decisions.

Schools can be about products, children who can read, write, are numerate and well behaved. Some would argue that is precisely what schools are for. Others would argue, with great emotion, that the most successful products are the outcome of a very long process, which is anything but superficial and takes years to come to fruition. Badley favours the second view. He believes that educational growth can only come from children themselves (see *Theme* 6). In this he is entirely in agreement with Froebel. In his view it is, for example, through questioning rules and their ethics that children come to impose on themselves self-control and community spirit, alongside individual creativity. Here we are touching on the recurring theme of unity which is explored in *Theme* 6. This leads to a consideration of school discipline. Badley's view of discipline as a long and continuous process of gradual development from external authority to increased degrees of responsible self-government. This is thought provoking, particularly his view that government eventually ceases to be necessary.

He is not suggesting that children should be left untutored, with no moral guidance. If their basic desire to be good is cultivated, they must be helped by those with more experience and understanding of life, and knowledge of the requirements of society. Hence, the adult is an external authority who gradually enables the growing child to take more and more part and eventually reaches self-government as an autonomously moral and good adult. This view hints towards the influence of Freud, Freud's theory of the Id, Ego and Super-Ego, which was a strong theoretical influence at this time. Children were seen to absorb the morals of the parent figure through the Super-Ego.

It may be that without the benefit of more recent research Badley has made the process of developing autonomous moral values or actions too much like one that begins in the earliest years of a child's life, with moulding and habit formation, and does not credit tiny children with enough ability to tackle weighty moral issues. Weston and Turiel (in Donaldson, Grieve and Pratt, 1983, pp. 62–5) demonstrated how young children can distinguish between social rules and moral principles. Children in this study had established a value: 'hitting to hurt is wrong'. They can distinguish between this and changing a social rule about tidying away toys.

This brings into question Badley's argument that nursery schools are what he calls places of 'the benevolent despotism'. He is certainly right in suggesting that most uninitiated visitors to nursery schools and classes see 'little visible evidence of the machinery of government'. He is also correct in suggesting that everything is planned and carried forward by the staff for the good of the children. However, it is more sophisticated than helping children to develop good habits. The way the curriculum is presented, the way adults talk to the children and encourage them to think through moral matters, is more than benevolent despotism. Right from the start, adults working in nursery education settings are helping children to understand rules, their purpose, function, how to make rules and good ways of carrying them out, whether cooking and eating together, or while playing in the home corner.

Another research study from the 1980s suggests that children can be helped from a very young age to do things, not for the admiration of adults and peers but because they are worth doing. Dweck and Legett (1988) distinguished between learning goals and achievement goals. Learning goals encourage autonomy and active thinking on the part of the child. Achievement goals lead to dependency on the admiration of others, and a tendency to give those in authority what they want. This has serious implications in the long term as to whether or not children are able to be autonomously good or bad. Believing in yourself brings higher self-esteem than depending on the admiration of others. Delinquent adolescents are noted for their low self-esteem. This suggests that approaches based on habit forming are inappropriate at nursery or any level of education, because they emphasise products of moral behaviour, which may not be attached, in synchrony with or matched to moral values. Products need to be linked with processes, or they float about unsupported and are easily swayed and toppled when the going gets tough. Badley is of this view when working with children of statutory school age. He would probably be moved to modify his view of the need for benevolent despotism for young children if he knew of more than the Freudian theory available then, and could make use of the recent interactionist research and theory quoted in this chapter.

There is, however, no need to update his views on extrinsic reward. No matter what the age of the child, he would be against it. He thinks that children who perform for carrots, stars, smiley faces, house points or silver cups are stunted, and perhaps even permanently dulled in their educational growth. Children in such a system of education become passive learners, dutiful but not moral. A teacher working in a school using extrinsic rewards suggested the pupils might find a book interesting in relation to the topic under study. The children asked, 'Will we get a mark for it?' When told they would not, the class lost interest.

Badley makes an emotive distinction between moulding children into moral shapes in the barrack-room according to a military pattern, or cultivating their goodness in a beautiful garden where there is creativity, caring, a sense of friendliness and community. In reality it is not as simple as this, for who in their right mind, if they love children, would opt for barracks when they could have a garden? It is in fact quite possible to be kind and warm to children, and still be in the business of habit formation and extrinsic reward.

Children can be turned into dutiful cogs in a machine quite humanely. The real problem is how to produce children who become adults who are both able to make and act appropriately on moral decisions. Cogs in a machine tend to depend on higher authority to make decisions for them. They are only as moral as others encourage them to be. Consequently, everything depends on the moral climate in which such children function. However the real difference between the barracks and the garden is the difference between product and processes. The product can only be as good as the processes which form it.

Consideration of who should control the choice about whether children are good or bad: should it be parents, religious groups, schools or central government?

Whether or not children are seen to be fundamentally inclined towards goodness or badness will have an impact on the way they are brought up, as well as the way an education system is organised. In the UK before the introduction in 1872 of a state education system compelling all children from 5 to 13 years of age to attend school, the question of intrinsic goodness or badness of humans was mainly a matter of concern for parents and organised religion. However, with the establishment of state schools, professionally trained teachers became central figures in the debate.

It is true that often the Christian church remained involved, with many schools having a church foundation and church control. A few Jewish schools were also permitted in the state sector. However, Badley demonstrates the way that lay educators, by 1938, when he published the article, had come to see their role as important in tackling the recurring theme of whether or not children are naturally inclined to goodness or badness. Badley says: 'it is we [teachers] who are responsible for the choice, for the question will be settled ultimately not on the battleground, but in the school.' He is obviously influenced by the atmosphere of the impending war in Europe, evidenced by his use of war imagery.

Froebel placed great emphasis on parents as educators, but believed they needed to be constantly supported by their community, helped by the teachers in schools which were part of the community. He believed that parents and teachers need to work closely together, in partnership. He thought that each, using their love and knowledge, could help the other to gain insights into the learning of the child.

In the 1930s children were handed over to schools for experts to teach them, but the partnership between state and parent was a benign one. As we have moved through the years since state education was first introduced in the UK, there have been fluctuations in the amount of control teachers could exert. Badley is writing just before the Second World War, when teachers led the first recurring theme. The same was true after this war, in the 1940s when progressive education was gradually introduced through the 1950s and 1960s, albeit in small pockets of the country.

We remember Froebel, Montessori, McMillan and Isaacs because they helped us to value both children as good and the adults close to them wanting to be and trying their best. At other times, central government has exerted more control as an outcome of the belief that those who teach them cannot be relied on, and that structures must give accountability a high priority in order to mould goodness from the outside.

The thinking behind the Code of Payment by Results (Revised Code 1862) was to use examinations in an attempt to improve standards in elementary education and in the belief that this is would help children from working class backgrounds. More detail of this is given by Liebschner (1991, p. 44).

The same emphasis on ensuring everyone in the education system, governors, staff and children, through external central government control and accountability mechanisms, is evident in the period of the late 1980s and 1990s. There has been a drastic reduction in the power of local education authorities, the introduction of a National Curriculum, standard assessment tasks, published league tables of results and increased inspections. No matter whether it is parents, religious leaders, teachers, local councils or central governments who control whether children are to be treated as intrinsically good or bad, the recurring theme does not go away, and never will in all probability.

SUMMARY

In this chapter, Badley's article has been examined in four ways:

1. It has explored what it means to be a good or bad person.
2. It has looked at whether or not limits need to be set, even if it is believed that children are fundamentally good.
3. It has involved looking at both the distinction and relationship between processes of moulding or cultivating and how these have an impact on the product of being a good or bad person.

4. Lastly it has explored who should make and act on decisions about whether or not children are inherently good or bad.

At times, Badley argues from a narrowly 1930s' viewpoint. However, he often shows a framework of thinking which is capable of moving back in time to meet and be in tune with Froebel's ideas and moving forwards to anticipate or clash with the present. This is because he has touched on a recurring theme in education.

Badley has been of assistance in this first chapter in demonstrating the needs and ways of re-exploring, reframing and restating the Froebelian belief in the fundamental goodness of children, in ways which are forward looking.

In the next chapter, the recurring theme changes from addressing the age-old question: 'Are children fundamentally good?' to another time-honoured and recurring question: 'What is the process of development?' An important part of this theme will be the subtext which asks, 'and does knowing about it matter anyway?' This book takes the stance that it does matter and, more than that, argues that being informed about it and able to act on knowledge and understanding of child development is central to the learning and teaching processes.

So far in this book we have looked at *Theme 1* – are children fundamentally good? Now we look at *Theme 2* – what is the process of development?

THEME 2:

What is the Process of Development?

The child, the boy, the man, indeed, should know no other endeavour but to be at every stage of development wholly what this stage calls for. Then will each successive stage spring like a new shoot from a healthy bud; and, at each successive stage, he will with the same endeavour again accomplish the requirements of this stage: for only the adequate development of man at each preceding stage can effect and bring about adequate development at each succeeding later stage.

(Froebel, 1887, p. 30)

INTRODUCTION

The first theme, regarding the goodness or badness of children, needs to be linked with the changing state of understanding and knowledge the child has at certain points of growing up. The question what is child development, and does it help the learning and teaching process, is another equally important recurring theme which runs through education. Throughout history there has been debate about the part that development plays, and how great that contribution is or is not.

In this chapter it will become evident that in the early part of the century this was a relatively simple matter to explore. Developmental theory was in an embryonic state. The emphasis in studying it was on the unfolding and creation of an optimum environment made up of people as well as physical materials. Interactionism was a straightforward concept to grasp and apply. Froebelians in particular, supported by Froebel's principles of child development, were strong because of knowing about these, and gained respect as teachers of quality.

In the chapter following this, the recurring theme surrounding the importance of development and its part in learning becomes a more complex affair, requiring new strategies. This is because, as the century moved on, new theories of child development challenged old ones and emerged in abundance. In that chapter we shall see how the need for augmentation of the concept of what development is becomes of vital importance.

Three articles have been selected to introduce this chapter. The first article contains two very brief extracts from a lecture given by Margaret McMillan in 1905 at a conference of teachers. (The full lecture is kept in the archives.) The second and third articles appear almost in full. They are both referring to an educational experiment set up in 1935, when a school invited Susan Isaacs to help them in their work. These articles have been selected because they signal some key recurring issues about what development is and the contribution that knowledge and understanding of child development have made in the modern classroom. It is the way that such theories are put to use in the classrooms that matter as much as deciding what development is. Theories only come alive for educators if they have practical meaning. Froebelians have always worked on this premise.

It is useful to read these extracts and to use them as a backcloth when reading the narrative and commentary on the article which makes up the remainder of the chapter. Striving to understand child development has been a recurring theme, both in the early days of the teaching profession and, as the chapter after this one indicates, remains so, in spite of being challenged by political forces.

The article by Margaret McMillan shows how this generation of educators was struggling to understand the principles of development, and references are made directly to Froebel's work (in translation) and to the demonstration of those who worked closely with him. The articles about the work of Miss Boyce and Susan Isaacs show the importance of those with knowledge of child development and the sharing of this with classroom teachers. However, they demonstrate their respect to professionalism by empowering teachers to develop their own practice rather than dictating it to them. These articles are therefore about two strands which contribute to the recurring theme which asks about the process of development:

1. The first quite simply is seeking more knowledge and understanding of the development of the child and assumes this to be an important thing to try to do.
2. The second is the issue which debates whether teachers should be told by either experts or lay people operating outside the classroom how to work with children. It raises the issue of whether or not classroom practice should be developed by those doing the teaching facilitated by experts who make bridges across the knowledge they need to acquire in order to be in a position to do this.

This means discussion about the level of education of teachers. Those who do as others tell them do not require as much education as those who are expected to seek knowledge, use it and develop the practice with children, parents and the network of colleagues with whom they work:

> because young children do not protest in ways which no-one can fail to understand, it is easy for them to become the victims of people who think it does not really matter whether they have trained teachers, or have to change their teachers very often, or who will even pause to consider whether this or that form of organisation, however administratively convenient it may be, or however well suited to older children, is

really right for them. We need to be constantly asking ourselves not whether young children can 'take it' but whether it is the best we can do for their fullest development.

(Gardner, 1971, p. 3)

This approach requires education at least to graduate level, in order to compare, contrast, describe, analyse, interpret and decide what classroom practice to favour and own as a cohesive and effective philosophy of education. In the early days, until 1957, Froebel teachers took on a three-year training rather than the two years offered in other colleges. This emphasised the arts, especially literature, drama, music, art and dance, natural science and mathematics, together with knowledge and understanding of child development. The interweaving of theory with practice was a strong part of this. The experiment described by Miss Boyce and Susan Isaacs shows the importance of the ability to use child development theory rather than be used by it.

TRUE AND FALSE APPLICATIONS McMillan, M. (1905) True and false applications of Froebel's principles to the teaching of children over seven. *Child Life*, Vol. vii, no. 27, pp. 138–46 (a paper read at the conference of teachers held by the London County Council and the Froebel Society on 7 January 1905).

[. . .] Certainly the new light which modern science has thrown on the development of the brain in the earliest years of life justifies entirely the seriousness which Froebel regarded the earliest epoch of life; but however that might be the elucidation and the occupation of his principles to the teaching of older children has been left very much to the insight and genius of the pedagogues of the future.

And yet Froebel did not lay down certain laws and principles which if they have any value at all, are valid for pupils of all ages and for schools of all kinds. It is our misfortune that he was not a writer, and he himself very frankly admits that he was never able quite successfully to expound his own system. We must remember, too, that the science of neurology, which has made such rapid strides in the last thirty years, was comparatively little developed in his day; and for this and other reasons his message was somewhat crippled. And yet the main lines of his teaching stand clearly out, and have borne the test of time.

There are three principles which he laid down which form the basis of his whole system. The first of these was this: that the child is a germinating centre – that he is part of a larger life, that he is a 'part-whole', as indeed, Froebel is continually calling him; that he is connected with something that is larger and yet identified with himself. That is his first great principle.

The second is the great principle of opposites. Education, said Froebel, is a kind of throbbing between contrasts – a movement between opposites and poles; and therefore in your curriculum and every subject there should appear a kind of antagonism that is bound to become a unity.

The third great principle was the connective principle, which he called the great law of the universe, in virtue of which all differences are reconciled, and all sciences find as it were one origin . . . .

Those three great principles of germinating life, of antagonism and of unity, appear according to Froebel wherever there is true education, and in an inviolate order and correlation . . .

She finishes her speech with a plea that teachers do not use strategies to excuse themselves from action on behalf of getting things right educationally for the child to develop and learn. She acknowledges how difficult it is to create the conditions needed for children to learn optimally:

But you will say how are our Authorities to supply these extraordinary conditions? Can they do anything in the direction of conditions that bring forth the best in intellectual life? If they cannot, so much the worse for England; but, as a matter of fact, the Authorities are not quite so bad as they are painted. I have been a member of one so I am very sensitive about Authorities, and I do not like to hear teachers say that they have to struggle against tremendous odds. No, the Authorities are not all bad; they are not a dead weight to be lifted. On the contrary, on every Education Committee in the country there are men and women who are doing their very best to assist in the realisation of the finest ideals. . .

In the final part of her speech to the audience she says:

It is you teachers – not the Authorities, but teachers – who have to put these things right. You are not as wax. If you are anything at all you are professionals, and if you are not professionals you are of no use as educationalists. The teacher who is worth anything is not to be driven, neither is he to be led blindly. It takes the teachings of the highest level of thought, but you must not interpret them slavishly. You know very well if you have listened to what has been said in this room today, that Froebel made 100 mistakes, that he was ignorant of many things that should be familiar to the least informed pupil-teacher in your school. He did not come here to tell you the whole truth.

AN EDUCATIONAL EXPERIMENT Boyce, E. (1935) An educational experiment. Play, work and the bridge between. *Child Life*, May, pp. 66–7.

To make an experiment, one must have a theory and also the substances on which to put it to the test. In chemistry this is easy, in education it is not so at all. We alluded in our last issue to the difficulties of getting the psychologist (or theorist) into the school, where alone he can be faced with the thousand and one difficulties of the real situation; and we spoke, too, of the desire among many teachers for his guidance. If only it could be got in 'realist' surroundings.

A very interesting episode has recently happened in St. Pancras. The Local Inspector, Mr. Pegrum was anxious to see practical demonstrations of methods in the Infant School, and to have some discussion with the local teachers of the questions which ought to be raised after any such demonstration. Moreover, the matter was to be thoroughly thrashed out in its psychological values.

The problem – play

Here the scientist was needed. Dr. Susan Isaacs was approached, and she was willing to co-operate. It was decided to review the work carried on in an Infant School – not an experimental school, but a progressive one – where it could be the basis of frank discussion, and offer something concrete as debatable ground. The main trend of debate was resumed by the title, 'Play Activities as a Basis of Formal Work'.

The Burghley Infant School, Tufnell Park, was chosen to be the 'body' for the experiment. The 'Burghley' School is a large one in a good working-class neighbourhood; it consists of 12 classes, with children from 4 years old to 7. The lower classes are 'play' classes; at about 6 years old, a child passes into the Transition stage, where formal work really beings, and the top of the school can be described as a place of formal work. As a preliminary, Dr. Isaacs spent a whole session in the school. She went from class to class as an ordinary visitor and spectator, without comment, merely to see what was going on.

Her visit was followed by an afternoon meeting, to which came about a hundred local teachers of children under eight years of age. Dr. Isaacs was introduced by Mr. Pegrum, and then spoke upon the Essentials of the Curriculum, and methods of carrying them out. Her speech rammed home the psychological values of the play curriculum. She stressed two points in particular: that the school-class should be a nursery, that is, a place of play, real play, where all sorts of materials are provided and used by the child for his own purposes – that it is worthwhile to let a child play till six years of age; and secondly, that the teacher must be a trained observer, able to watch quietly. The importance of this play is the fact that play which seemed to be 'just a muddle' often gave the clue to the hidden emotional or intellectual difficulties of the child. Lastly, she discussed different kinds of play – washing the dolls, tea parties, cooking – with real pastry! – which she considers most valuable, and so on to the practical details of clearing up, with plenty of time.

A concrete case

This meeting was followed by three visits made by the teachers in three groups to the 'Burghley'. Each group saw three classes at their play activities, three in the Transition stage, where formal work emerges, and then visited the highest classes. Neither children nor staff were in the least disturbed by the numbers of visitors.

Thus there was a wide field opened up for discussion. It was understood that discussion was to be frank and fearless. Two main points which clearly must

Mathematics, Science and Technology: 1990s

come up were the actual value of the play occupations, and again, the all important question of the sufficiency of the 'Bridge' or Transition way to formal work.

In the Transition classes, play has to be taken more thoroughly. A notion arises, however direct from the play, to support more serious work. In the game of shops, the shops require prices for the goods, bills were needed, and money had to be added and subtracted. Consequently number, and even the formal setting down of sums, became a necessity. And from the 'academic' point of view, the question must arise, at the end of it all, can the children really read and write and do arithmetic?

The pros and cons

About a month after these visits, at a date unavoidably rather late, Mr. Pegrum arranged the Discussion Meeting, which was necessary to the scheme. It was limited purposely to those who had visited the school. Miss F. Roe, the Head Mistress of the 'Burghley' spoke first, as she had been asked to speak to clarify the aims of the school. Dr. Isaacs was also present, to answer questions and discuss criticisms and theories. Written questions and remarks had been sent in beforehand. The aim of the discussion was to get down to the principle of the thing.

And, of course, the first main, unavoidable question was, can't the children do this sort of thing at home and do real work at school? To this Dr. Isaacs answer was definite. It is just because this place is school that the children must

Mathematics, Science and Technology: 1940s

play here. There is not time nor room nor material at home for cooking, hammering, messing about and making a muddle for mother to clear up. Nor is there always the companionship of the many others.

A great many practical difficulties were brought forward by different speakers. For example, the need for space, in work of this kind, and again, the noise made by hammering etc. which children who are really playing freely are sure to want to make. In answer to this, it was pointed out that times can be made when noise is permissible, and other times when it is not, on the principle that some degree of co-operation and restraint is natural and desirable.

The discussion covered much other ground. Perhaps for want of time, the question of the transition period did not come in for full examination. But everything cannot be done at once, and matter enough was handled in any case.

Two factors of value

We cannot follow the discussion out to its end. Nor is it important that we should. What is of more importance is to stress the conditions that make this piece of work so interesting. First, we would put the interaction of the teachers of one district with a scientist of established repute, on their home ground. Second, we would put the use of a school, doing its ordinary work in its own building, and offered freely as a basis for honest and unabashed argument, pro and con. The whole episode forms a notable example of collaboration between workers in two different spheres of education.

UNORGANISED PLAY Boyce, E. (1935) Unorganised play. *Child Life* (New Series), no. 6, and comment by Dr Isaacs

We watch the Nursery School child at play, and accept this sort of activity at this age as normal and desirable. But too often the five-to-six year old is expected to cease his play activities in school and to begin lessons. Yet some educationalists would like all children under seven to enjoy Nursery School conditions where play and living experiences are the accepted mode of learning.

Experiments are being carried out in various types of schools, and one such experiment I know well. The particular group of children I have in mind come from extremely poor homes. During their third and fourth years they were educated in the nursery class of an elementary school They are now between the ages of five and six years, and are still enjoying the free unorganised play of their earlier school years.

There are thirty-eight children in the group, boys and girls, the ages varying from 5 years 3 months to 5 years 10 months. The programme of the day is arranged so that half their time is spent in play and the other half in music, stories and verse, acting, washing and eating, cleaning and tidying their school-room, and going on expeditions.

The equipment of the room includes a playhouse, large enough to hold several children, and furnished with beds and dolls, equipped dresser, perambulator, little chairs and tables and tea sets. It includes also: large and small bricks, a deep sand trough, utensils for cooking and for washing clothes, clay and plasticine, scissors, pictures, paste, scales, weights and measures, materials and shelves for a shop, outfits for tram and bus drivers, postmen etc., tram and bus tickets, large low boards and chalks, brushes and paints, mosaics, bead games, coloured tablets, insets, gummed shapes etc., bench and tools for carpentry, picture books and sewing materials and a low nature table.

The conditions of play are these: the children are free to play in any way they like, but no aggressive or destructive behaviour is allowed. They are warned of 'clearing away' time and are trained to tidy and clean up after their play period. Some materials are so popular that turns have to be taken e.g. in using a mincing machine to grind crusts into crumbs for the birds. Groups for cooking are also organised, as this is such a popular activity.

Let us first observe 'Shopping'. The children began by experimenting with the weights and measures. They weighed stones, wooden bricks, cotton reels etc. They played at shopkeepers and customers, but without any real understanding of barter. They cut pieces of cardboard for money, but did not realise the significance of giving change. Often the shopkeeper insisted on giving money as well as goods to his customers.

Empty display packets were added to their stores, and these were arranged on 1d. or 2d. or 3d. shelves. To encourage correct exchange, the teacher often played with them. Later on they sold real things from jars, e.g. dried peas, haricot beans, etc. The teacher records that weighing was accurate a long time before right money was used. During the twelfth week of the term the play became decidedly more accurate. Many children now shop properly, and take their purchases back with them in the playhouse, enjoying parties, weddings, family excursions and hospital visits. In each case the food previously purchased plays a significant part in the family games.

'Mothers and fathers'

There are always children playing in the 'home'. Each morning the dolls are bathed and dressed, and play a prominent part in the day's activities. One little girl takes the babies out for their airing (in the corridor). When the 'mother' calls 'Mary come home!' she returns immediately and helps to prepare a meal for the 'babies'. Sometimes there is a sewing party in the house – they bring in their canvas and wool or dolls pieces and sit chatting together, while one makes 'tea' and another washes and irons little garments, or mends them with very large stitches. Any boy, conveniently near, is almost forced into being a father. He has to 'mend' the house, clean the shoes or take a significant part if a wedding is in progress. The teacher records: 'They order each other about, everyone trying to get his or her ideas accepted and carried out by the rest of the group'.

Sometimes one member of the groups say, 'we are going down to the seaside'. They buy a whole basket full of shopping, pack cups and saucers, dress up and get their dolls. They buy tickets and then wait for the bus, and go off to join a group or boys who have been busy with bricks. They all have tea

Mathematics, Science and Technology: 1900s

together and then come back 'home'. This is a ritualistic game which may be carried out for several days in succession.

Cooking and washing

The most popular activity is cooking, but its rival is washing. Dishes, wooden utensils, plates, tea sets, dolls and bed clothes all provide excuses for washing. Scrubbing brushes are constantly in demand – the cooking table needs scrubbing or the floor of the house. 'I must scrub' is the most repeated rejoinder when we try to dissuade them into a drier occupation. On a washing day they 'work fast and furiously with great concentration' (teacher's note) using miniature scrubbing boards and wringers. 'I'm quite out of breath', one remarks with satisfaction. Ironing with small warm irons also brings them satisfaction. Several times lately they have undertaken a complete wash of their dressing-up clothes.

The ingredients for cakes, tarts and puddings are provided for the children's use, and they can make what they like. Care and control in measuring and mixing has considerably increased since they first began. They decide beforehand what they will make – chocolate cakes, jam tarts, pancakes, etc. But they also experiment. 'I'm going to make an apple pie', cried Harry. After some time of absorbed attention, he soliloquised, 'I'll put in currants too'. Then, with a shout of excitement, 'I'll sprinkle it all with chocolate and sugar!' The finished goodies are eaten at a birthday feast, taken home as gifts, or sold on the 'coffee stall'. These are only some few of the numerous games played.

Constructive efforts of groups

After three months of play we noticed more efforts at co-operative construction. The first piece of successful co-operative play of this sort was a fire engine. The leader was a highly imaginative child who stimulated his friends during the making of a vivid red engine from an orange box. They had used carpenter's tools from the age of four, and previously had made daggers, ladders, guns, aeroplanes etc. When the engine was complete with its fire escape, they brought rubber tubing from home for the hose. There were many make believe fires, when the house and its occupants were either saved or destroyed. They discovered the principle of the hosepipe by fixing it to a tap out of doors. With the teacher's help, they organised this interest into a dramatic play with music.

The fire engine was the beginning of a series of similar efforts. The second was a fruit and vegetable barrow. Some of the parents are hawkers, and the depot for hiring barrows is actually next door to the school. Market garden produce was made by a second group of children, while five boys were engaged in barrow construction, and later in hawking. The first demand for writing names came when the barrow had to be decorated with the names of the proprietors. An enthusiasm for names began from that day, and almost every child asked for a copy of his own name, for those of the dolls, and for most of the well loved toys. The scales were carted round on the barrow, and the familiar cries of the street vendors echoed along corridors. The older children in the school, who were building 'Covent Garden' volunteered to bring their 'horse and cart' laden with vegetables to supply the growing needs of the hawkers.

The third and fourth group efforts began simultaneously – a Green Line coach and a train. The completed vehicles each accommodate a driver and a passenger. The greatest problem was concerned with steering gear. They tinkered about with pieces of wire, wood, cotton reels and nails until something resembling a 'starter' was fixed. There are three stages, each costing 1d. The little passenger holds tight and stops at each traffic signal until at last Southend (a sand pit) is reached. The favourite play in sand is to build bridges, tunnels, castles, or to dig out and fill in paddling pools.

The latest group efforts has been a coffee stall, where a workman can buy a cup of tea or coffee. The results of their cooking activities are now generally sold at this stall. The barter is accurate, the stall-holder countering his profit and attempting to record it.

Reading and writing

The first enthusiasm for the written word occurred when the children wanted to see their own names. The commodities in the shop were also labelled for them. At the end of February, when the average age of the children was about 5½ years, there began a keen interest in writing. During the play periods whole groups of children settled down at writing tables with coloured pencils and 'names' clamouring for help and approval. By the middle of March half the children voluntarily played with names, unhooking and hooking them up again, finding the names of their friends, and matching dolls to their names. When the coffee stall was finished, they dictated the notices e.g. 'Hot coffee', 'Good tea', 'Open' etc. and now use these as copies or as games when they are playing 'school'.

It is not surprising that this group contains the older members of the class. They also pore over picture books in the quiet room, and take a great interest in the reading activities of the older children in the school. The rest of the class show no desire at present to join in these enthusiasms.

Estimate of number knowledge

No attempt whatever is made to encourage the children to write figures. But many of them do copy any figures that are displayed in the shop. They sort out the tram and bus tickets, and can pay correct money for whichever ticket they need. By this time too, most of them pay accurately when shopping, and some give right change.